STEM IN SOCCER

CONNECTING STEM AND SPORTS

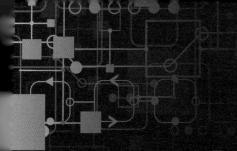

CONNECTING
STEM
AND SPORTS

STEM IN SOCCER

JACQUELINE HAVELKA

MASON CREST
PHILADELPHIA · MIAMI

Mason Crest
450 Parkway Drive, Suite D
Broomall, Pennsylvania 19008
(866) MCP-BOOK (toll free)

First printing
9 8 7 6 5 4 3 2 1

ISBN (hardback) 978-1-4222-4337-4
ISBN (series) 978-1-4222-4329-9
ISBN (ebook) 978-1-4222-7481-1

Cataloging-in-Publication Data on file with the Library of Congress

Developed and Produced by National Highlights Inc.
Editor: Andrew Luke
Interior and cover design: Annalisa Gumbrecht, Studio Gumbrecht
Production: Michelle Luke

QR CODES AND LINKS TO THIRD-PARTY CONTENT

You may gain access to certain third-party content ("Third-Party Sites") by scanning and using the QR
Codes that appear in this publication (the "QR Codes"). We do not operate or control in any respect any
information, products, or services on such Third-Party Sites linked to by us via the QR Codes included in
this publication, and we assume no responsibility for any materials you may access using the QR Codes.
Your use of the QR Codes may be subject to terms, limitations, or restrictions set forth in the applicable
terms of use or otherwise established by the owners of the Third-Party Sites. Our linking to such Third-
Party Sites via the QR Codes does not imply an endorsement or sponsorship of such Third-Party Sites
or the information, products, or services offered on or through the Third-Party Sites, nor does it imply an
endorsement or sponsorship of this publication by the owners of such Third-Party Sites.

TABLE OF CONTENTS

KEY ICONS TO LOOK FOR:

 Words To Understand: These words with their easy-to-understand definitions will increase the reader's understanding of the text while building vocabulary skills.

 Sidebars: This boxed material within the main text allows readers to build knowledge, gain insights, explore possibilities, and broaden their perspectives by weaving together additional information to provide realistic and holistic perspectives.

 Educational Videos: Readers can view videos by scanning our QR codes, providing them with additional educational content to supplement the text. Examples include news coverage, moments in history, speeches, iconic sports moments, and much more!

 Text-Dependent Questions: These questions send the reader back to the text for more careful attention to the evidence presented there.

 Research Projects: Readers are pointed toward areas of further inquiry connected to each chapter. Suggestions are provided for projects that encourage deeper research and analysis.

 Series Glossary Of Key Terms: This back-of-the-book glossary contains terminology used throughout this series. Words found here increase the reader's ability to read and comprehend higher-level books and articles in this field.

INTRODUCTION

Macaroni and cheese. Texting and emojis. STEM and sports. What? STEM . . . and sports? Yes! These are things that naturally fit together. When people talk about STEM classes and sports, they are usually viewed as opposite things, right? You're either sitting in class learning science and math, or you're out on the field participating in sports.

But STEM and sports do go together. STEM is education in four specific areas—science, technology, engineering, and mathematics. STEM curriculum is integrated for real-world learning. Think of a class taking a field trip to an amusement park. Students learn the principles of physics. For example, Newton's laws of physics apply to soccer.

- ◇ Newton's First Law: An object at rest stays at rest. To move, an external force must act on it. A soccer ball resting on the penalty spot will stay there until the shooter kicks it. This defines the law of inertia.

- ◇ Newton's Second Law of Motion defines the *F=ma* equation. This law says that the force of an object is equal to its mass multiplied by its acceleration. The harder the quarterback throws the ball, the more force it has.

- ◇ Newton's Third Law of Motion states that for every action, there is an equal and opposite reaction. So, after the touchdown, the harder you spike the ball into the ground, the higher up into the air it will go.

There's lots of science in soccer. Let's take a look at the STEM concepts behind some of soccer's greatest plays. We'll explore all the concepts like force, inertia, and acceleration, which are important to the game of soccer.

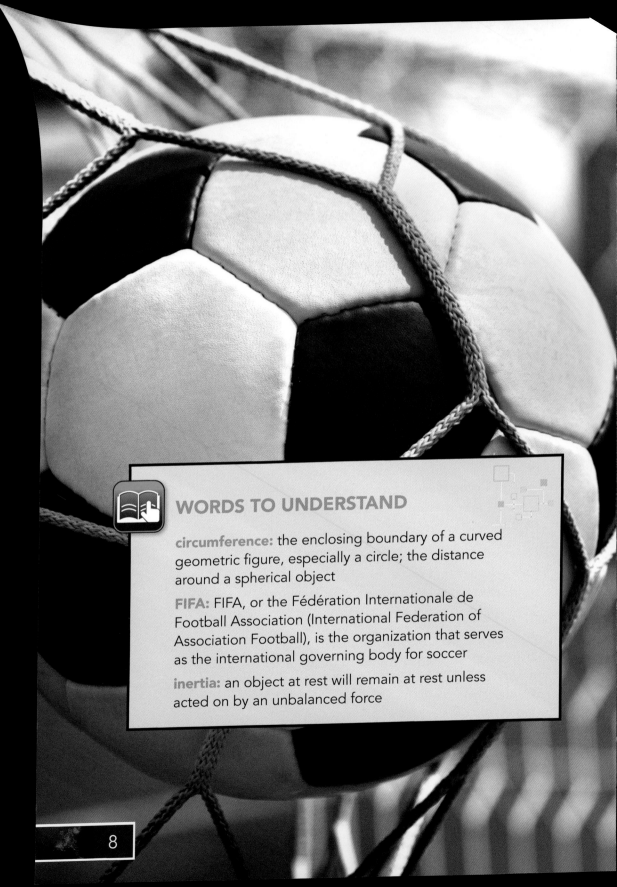

WORDS TO UNDERSTAND

circumference: the enclosing boundary of a curved geometric figure, especially a circle; the distance around a spherical object

FIFA: FIFA, or the Fédération Internationale de Football Association (International Federation of Association Football), is the organization that serves as the international governing body for soccer

inertia: an object at rest will remain at rest unless acted on by an unbalanced force

CHAPTER 1

FORCES THAT ACT ON A SOCCER BALL

Soccer is a complex sport, but you probably never thought of soccer as having complex physics. Many different forces affect a soccer ball. Think about the *F=ma* equation—*force* is equal to *mass* times *acceleration*. This means that the more the ball weighs, the harder it is to kick.

Soccer balls range in size from 1 to 5, as measured by the ball's **circumference**. The largest ball is size 5 and is used by all leagues for players age twelve or over, including high school teams, college teams, semiprofessional teams, and in the professional ranks of Major League Soccer (MLS) and Fédération Internationale de Football Association (**FIFA**).

A size 5 ball is about twenty-eight inches in circumference and weighs between fourteen and sixteen ounces (420 to 450 grams), or about a pound. (As a side note, the ball is weighed before each match but can actually weigh more during

A soccer ball will stay at rest until acted on by a kicker.

the match if it absorbs dirt and moisture.) The ball's inflatable bladder, lining, leather cover, and stitching all affect its weight.

Newton's Laws and Soccer

Newton's law of **inertia** states that an object at rest will remain at rest unless an unbalanced force (in this case, the kicker) acts on it. Therefore, the $F=ma$ equation applies in this case, and the force of the kick is the major force acting on the ball. The value of m is the mass of the soccer ball, and F is the amount of force the kicking or throwing player uses. Acceleration (a) is produced when a force acts on a mass. It is now easy to see why FIFA wants to control the mass of the ball, right?

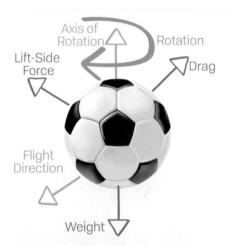

Eventually, of course, the soccer ball does stop, hopefully in the goal. Newton's law of motion comes into play here: An object in motion continues in motion with the same speed and in the same direction unless acted on by an unbalanced force.

Gravity, drag, and friction are also forces that act on the soccer ball. Gravity pulls the ball down toward the ground as the ball is in flight. Friction is the force that acts on the ball as it moves over the playing surface, such as grass or a hard artificial surface. Friction occurs as two surfaces (the ball and the field) make contact with each other. As the soccer ball rubs against the ground, a resistance in movement occurs to help slow the ball down. Drag is the force of the air pushing on the ball as it travels in flight. Think of drag as air friction. The air around the ball helps slow it down.

The Magnus Effect

Can a player do anything to reduce the forces on the ball? Soccer players know this trick—kicking the ball off center. When a ball is kicked off center, the ball will begin to spin, and the direction as well as the speed of the spin determines how much the ball will curve as it flies through the air. It is the same principle that occurs in baseball when the pitcher throws a curve ball. This effect is known as the Magnus effect. German physicist Gustav Magnus first described the spinning effect in 1852 when he was trying to determine why spinning bullets deflected to one side or the other.

What are the physics behind the Magnus effect? The off-center kick initiates the spin, and as the ball goes through the air, the drag (friction between the ball and the air) causes the air to react to the spin direction. The ball is moving forward at the same time it is spinning, and the spin makes the air flow faster on one side of the ball. Let's say the soccer player kicks the ball to the right of the center; this will cause the ball to spin counterclockwise.

Players try to use the Magnus effect to their advantage when taking free kicks.

The Magnus forces act left so the ball curves to the left. When the ball is kicked left of center, the ball spins clockwise, and the Magnus force causes the ball to curve to the right.

A ball kicked directly on center will travel in a particular straight trajectory. A ball kicked to the left or the right can result in a Magnus effect that lands the ball several feet from that original trajectory. This maneuver is commonly known as "bending the ball." It is an effective strategy that soccer players use when attempting to score goals because it is much harder for the goalie to predict what the ball's path will be.

Can a player's corner kick result in a goal? See the Magnus effect in action!

Interestingly, initially in the kick, the ball will go straight without spinning because it is traveling very quickly and therefore has less air resistance. As the ball slows down, the airflow will cause it to begin bending. You'll notice that the slower the ball goes, the more it will spin or curl.

Soccer players have other moves, too, like putting a backspin on the ball. This means air will move faster at the top of the ball than at the bottom, causing the ball to rise more and therefore travel further.

A corner kick into the net demonstrates the Magnus effect at its finest, but just how is this done? How does a player *Bend It Like Beckham*, as the famous movie title exhorts? Many players are very good at kicking the ball off center; that provides the bend or curve to the right or left. But players usually struggle with kicking the ball in precisely the right direction with the power needed to propel the ball where it needs to land—in the net.

David Beckham is a former English soccer star who was famous for his ability to make the ball bend in midair.

This type of corner kick is called an Olympic goal, or *gól Olímpico*. It was so named after a 1924 friendly soccer match between reigning Olympic champion Argentina and archrival Uruguay. Argentine striker Cesareo Onzari fired a corner kick that spun directly into the goal, and the play was forever dubbed *gól Olímpico*.

Nearly 100 years later, very few players have managed the kick during a match. In 2012, US Women's National team star Megan Rapinoe scored one by accident, meaning to place the ball a few yards in front of the goal so that her teammate could score. The kick curved left and actually went through the legs of an opposing team member, and then it bounced by Canada's goalie and right into the net. That same year, French star Thierry Henry scored an Olympic goal in an MLS match. And in 2018, another Argentine, Angel di Maria, scored one for his French club side, Paris Saint-Germain.

FIFA's Mission to Stop Match Fixing

In 2012, FIFA launched the FIFA Integrity Initiative, a zero-tolerance policy against match fixing. The initiative focuses on intelligence-gathering and detection of potential match manipulation. FIFA uses state-of-the-art software technology and analytics to monitor FIFA matches worldwide. The software identifies irregular activity in the sports-betting market. That irregular activity usually is an indication of match manipulation. An expert in-house team helps FIFA with this analysis. These experts monitor sports bets, detect fraud, and monitor hacking attempts at 211 worldwide FIFA-affiliated clubs and teams.

If you've ever tried to kick this type of goal, or if you watch the above video link, when you see the physics involved it is easy to understand why you rarely see Olympic goals. Only players with the utmost confidence and technical ability would even attempt such a shot. Much of the difficulty lies in plane geometry and in line of sight. The corner of the field is in the same plane as the goal, so the player is literally trying to hit a target he or she cannot see. In a professional match, the chances that no other player will touch the ball are slim to none. Finally, players know that the environment affects the flight path; factors like altitude, wind speed, and even humidity play a role. For all these reasons, and because players get only one shot, fans don't see Olympic goals because the risk of missing the shot is simply too high. Instead, the player typically places the ball in front of the goal.

If a player were to attempt this kind of kick, the only way to succeed is to create major spin on the ball. American soccer great Brandi Chastain says you make the ball turn the way you want to depending on how your foot contacts the ball during the kick. She says that if a player shoots from the left corner, the trick is to kick about two inches below the ball's midline on the ball's right side. This foot placement gives the ball loft as well as a wicked counterclockwise spin around the ball's vertical axis. If you kick it correctly, you should feel the force in the big knobby bone of your big toe (called the first metatarsal).

Air moves over the ball as it is in flight. There is air moving counterclockwise, or with the spin, and air moving clockwise, flowing against the ball. For the air moving with the spin, a thin layer of turbulence creates drag on the air to deflect the air back behind itself. Newton's Third Law dictates that this air will deflect the ball in the opposite direction but with equal force, and that creates the bend.

To score an Olympic goal, this player would have to curve the ball directly into the net off this corner kick.

The Magnus effect applies to other sports like golf and baseball, but it can also apply to much bigger objects. For instance, did you know that the Magnus effect is used to propel sea tankers? Amazingly, these ships have ten-story-tall metal cylinders that spin to create the Magnus effect to move the ship forward.

Ball Surface

If you've looked at a soccer ball up close, you know it is traditionally designed from hexagonal-shaped panels that are stitched together. Why are soccer balls built this way? Wouldn't it be easier to have a ball with a smooth surface?

A much smaller ball for a different sport is designed in the same way. Golf balls have a dimpled surface because the dimpling actually increases the air resistance to make a much more pronounced spinning effect. A dimpled soccer ball has the same principle.

One thing that golf balls and soccer balls have in common is that in both cases, contact with the ball, whether from a golf club or a soccer player's foot, is very, very brief. However, that contact establishes several important factors, including velocity, spin rate, and launch angle. After the kick, gravity and aerodynamics control the ball, and that is why the design of the surface of the soccer ball is so important.

The raised hexagonal pattern on a soccer ball helps it counter the force of drag as it travels through the air.

If a soccer ball were smooth, it would travel only about half as far as a soccer ball with the hexagonal surface (some golf balls are made with the same hexagonal dimples as a soccer ball). Any object traveling through the air has drag and lift forces exerted on it. Drag is a force that directly opposes motion, whereas lift is a force that acts perpendicular to the motion of the ball. In a soccer ball, lift is directed upward. As the ball rotates in the air, the amount and direction of lift and drag vary. The indentations in the soccer ball create a thin layer of air (called a boundary layer) that clings to the surface of the ball and decreases drag. As a soccer ball spins, the air pressure on the bottom of the ball is higher than on the top, and, therefore, the ball lifts in the air.

The surface of the ball can also influence its flight: The rougher the ball, the more pronounced the Magnus effect. If a soccer ball's surface were perfectly smooth, the air drag on the ball has a harder time dragging in the direction of the spin. The turbulence would form around the side of the ball moving against the air flow rather than the side moving with the air flow. The effect on the ball would be to deflect in the direction that is opposite to the ball's spin. Interestingly, a smoother ball actually produces a reverse Magnus effect.

Text-Dependent Questions:

1. Do all of Newton's laws apply to a kicked soccer ball? How?

2. How does the mass of the soccer ball affect how fast it goes?

3. How does Newton's Third Law apply to off-center soccer ball kicks (Magnus effect)?

Research Project:

Do some *F=ma* calculations. For mass, initially use the mass of a FIFA size 5 regulation soccer ball (fourteen to sixteen ounces). Choose a force by which to kick the ball, and then determine what the acceleration will be given that mass and force. Vary different masses and forces to determine how those changes affect the acceleration of the ball. Record your observations in a notebook. How do changes in mass and force affect the acceleration?

WORDS TO UNDERSTAND

kinetic energy: kinetic energy is the energy of motion. An object that has motion—whether it is vertical or horizontal motion—has kinetic energy; translational kinetic energy refers to energy created by moving from one location to another location

piston: A piston is a sliding piece moved by or moving against fluid pressure, as in an engine. The piston is a short cylindrical body that fits within a cylindrical chamber or vessel along which it moves back and forth

potential energy: potential energy is the energy that a piece of matter has because of its static position

CHAPTER 2

THE PHYSICS OF KICKING A SOCCER BALL

Great soccer players are experts at kicking, and, perhaps unwittingly, they work on scientific principles to modify their kicks for any given situation that might occur in a match. Simply changing the physics of the sport can have dramatic effects on the course of a match.

What are the physics behind kicking? As the player's foot comes into contact with the ball, an energy called kinetic energy is transferred to the ball. The physics equation for **kinetic energy** is

$$K=1/2 \ mv2$$

Physics of a Kick

The mass of the player's body (*m*) and the velocity (speed) at which the player kicks the ball (*v*) both determine how much energy is transferred to the ball. In fact, if you were to watch a kick in slow motion, you would actually see the ball deform. When the player's foot strikes the ball, the contact surface of the ball becomes flat for a microsecond. Remember that energy balance going in must equal the

Watch this soccer ball hit the man's face in slow motion. You can see the deformation of the ball and his face!

energy balance going out. Therefore, the energy going into the ball is the energy of the kick plus the stored (**potential**) **energy** in the ball. The energy out is the kinetic energy of the ball plus heat given off. The more the ball deforms, the more heat is in this energy balance.

Foot Forces

What forces are enacted on a soccer player's foot as he or she kicks the ball? For that, we can go back to our trusty *F=ma* equation. An average size 5 soccer ball weighs about 0.4 kilograms. A typical professional soccer kick has an acceleration of about 3,000 meters per second squared (m/s^2). Now, we can calculate the force. Multiplying 0.4 kg times 3,000 m/s^2 results in 1,200 kilograms m/s^2.

To convert that number into something a bit more meaningful, like weight, we can divide 1,200 by 9.8 m. Therefore, a professional soccer player experiences a weight of 122 kg of force on his leg. Considering the average American male weighs 87 kg, the force on the foot is more than the force of an entire person's weight.

The force on the foot of a pro soccer player when kicking the ball can be more than the force of his entire weight.

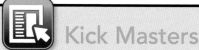 Kick Masters

Who are five of the greatest free-kick takers of all time?

David Beckham: Of course Beckham is one of the most well-known soccer players in the world and one of England's all-time best free-kick takers. Beckham is known for an amazing and memorable free-kick goal against Greece in the very last moments of the match to help England qualify for the 2002 FIFA World Cup. Goalkeepers feared him, because very few can bend it like Beckham.

Ronaldinho: He played for Brazil in the 1990s and 2000s and had many memorable goals including an amazing goal from forty yards (36.5 m) away to win the match and knock England out of the 2002 FIFA World Cup.

Roberto Carlos: He played for Brazil and was known for his free-kick precision and power. He made an amazing kick in a game against France in 1997. As fans watched, the ball seemed to be going wide, only to curl back inside the post and into the net.

Cristiano Ronaldo: The famous Portuguese player scores goals from every angle. And his free kicks win many games.

Lionel Messi: Many soccer experts agree that this player for Argentina is the best soccer player ever. Many regard Messi as one of the best free-kick takers in the world.

Does Height Matter?

Does the height of the soccer player matter when kicking the ball? Do taller players have an advantage? A common misconception in soccer is that the taller a player is, the harder that player will kick, but that isn't necessarily the case. As we see in the previous equation, the formula depends on the mass of the player's leg. Being taller doesn't necessarily mean you have more muscle mass in that leg. The equation also depends on the velocity of the ball, meaning how much energy a player puts into the kick—and that doesn't depend on height either. In the equation, velocity is squared, so the faster you kick the ball, the more it matters because of the compounding effect in the equation. It's all about leg power, which transfers into velocity. A shorter player may have more leg power and therefore may kick the ball harder, despite perhaps having slightly less leg mass than a taller player.

Lionel Messi, who is 5'7", is one of the sport's biggest stars, and proof that height does not matter in soccer.

For this reason, soccer players train on leg speed above all else. Any soccer coach will tell you that they put a priority on speed and agility training. Players train to hit the field with the balls of their feet first, and to angle their feet to hit the ground with maximum power. Coaches teach players how to drive their leg power with their hip muscles so the player's field position doesn't slow them down. Think of your knees functioning like **pistons**, moving up and down to propel your body forward down the field.

A good soccer kick requires very little follow through.

Maximizing Kick Power

If you play or watch tennis or baseball, coaches always want their players to follow through with the racket or the bat. Does the same apply to soccer? Can follow-through after you kick the ball help?

In soccer, the foot is in contact with the soccer ball for only a very slight amount of time (about 0.01 seconds). Any energy you use in a follow-through or in any other motion during or after the kick takes away from the energy transfer you put into the ball. Therefore, unlike in some other sports, follow-through is not desired in soccer because all the energy from your kick needs to be transferred into the ball.

Text-Dependent Questions:

1. What is the equation for kinetic energy?

2. Name two reasons why a soccer ball is designed with a hexagonal surface.

3. Would you rather be a shorter player with a stronger leg, or a taller player with a weaker leg? Why?

Research Project:

Here is a great project to test the theories of potential and kinetic energy. Drop a soccer ball from a height of six feet. Measure how high the soccer ball bounces after it hits the ground. Next, place a tennis ball over the soccer ball and drop both of them at the same time from a height of six feet. You will likely observe that the soccer ball doesn't bounce much, but the tennis ball will bounce very high. This is because the tennis ball is getting kinetic energy from itself as well as from the soccer ball. This is called the slingshot effect and is the same principle that NASA scientists use on satellites. Think of the soccer ball as a big planet and the tennis ball as a satellite. The satellite is sent very close to the surface of a big planet, using the planet's gravitational pull to gain kinetic energy to increase the speed of the satellite to slingshot around the planet.

WORDS TO UNDERSTAND

probability: the likelihood of a certain outcome happening in a set of all possible outcomes

psychologist: a person who studies the mental or behavioral characteristics of an individual or group

reaction time: the length of time between a stimulus and a person's response to it, that is, how fast a person reacts

CHAPTER 3

GOALIE SCIENCE

GOOOOOOOOOOOOOAL!!!!!!! This is the call all fans love to hear. The only person who doesn't enjoy hearing it is the other team's goalie. How does a player become a good goalie? Are taller players better goalies? Are players with a bigger arm span better goalies? Or do players with the fastest **reaction times** make the best goalies? Let's explore.

Man vs. Net Area

Penalty kicks are hard to stop, and lots of factors of physics are behind why that is the case. First, a soccer goal is very large. At a length of twenty-four feet and a height of eight feet, the soccer goal has a total area of 192 square feet. To put it in perspective, the net is larger than a cargo container. During a penalty kick, the opponent stands thirty-six feet away from the net. The kicker can choose to land that ball anywhere in that cargo container space. It's all about time—the kicker can kick the ball much faster than the goalie can react.

Human reaction time, even for the quickest of goalkeepers or those with the biggest arm span, is simply not fast enough to

Limited by human reaction time, the goalkeeper is at a significant disadvantage on penalty kicks.

cover that amount of area for a ball kicked that quickly. Let's do the math.

The formula for velocity (speed) is straightforward—distance over time. To calculate it, distance is the target position minus the starting position, in this case, thirty-six feet. An average penalty kick has a speed of seventy miles per hour. Therefore, knowing the speed and the distance, it is easy to calculate the time it takes for the kick to occur. It takes the ball less than half a second to reach the net. The goalkeeper has about 700 milliseconds to look at the ball, decide where it is going, and react, but in reality, it takes the goalkeeper about a second. The kicker always has the advantage. The only way the goalie has an edge is if they move before the kick, and that is what most of them do. It all comes back to the law of **probability**.

Think Fast

Reaction time also plays a big part in whether the goalie will make the play. Measurements indicate that it can take as much as a whole second for the goalkeeper to watch and react to the ball by moving in its direction. Unfortunately, by then, the goal is already scored, so goalies need a reaction time that is as fast as possible.

Genetics certainly play a part. For example, males have faster reaction times than females. Age is a factor. In general, reaction times slow as a person gets older. Researchers who have studied reaction time have learned that reaction time gets faster until people reach age thirty, then it starts to slowly decrease. Children have slower reaction times. If you're tired, or ill, or on certain medications, your reaction time will also be negatively affected. Furthermore, distraction from another player or by fans can also slow reaction times. This is why the noise level in a stadium or air horns going off in the stadium can be effective. People who are anxious or have taken in moderate amounts of caffeine have faster reaction times.

But genetics don't play the whole role. Training matters. Reaction times definitely shorten with training. Reaction time depends on developing the muscles to have more force, strength, and power. Most professional goalies will tell you that practice does make perfect. When you train to react to the ball, your muscles build memory function. Soccer is a high-speed sport, and a player's reflexes are definitely important—the

Look at these incredible goalie saves! Wow!

quicker, the better. In fact, reaction time often determines the game's outcome. Look in chapter 5 for more details about how to improve reaction time.

The Mental Game

If a goalie can't physically cover the whole net, is there a way he or she can know which direction the player will kick the ball? Recall the Magnus effect from chapter 2. Is there a way a goalie can tell whether the kicker is going to kick the ball off-center left or right?

This is where goalie preparation—both physical and mental—comes into play. Goalies certainly study video footage of their opposing teams. They learn the habits of the players and how those players are most likely going to kick the ball. In this case, soccer becomes a game of probability. Research conducted in London at Brunel University indicated that in 70 percent of the cases, skilled goalkeepers guessed correctly regarding how a penalty kick would go down. However, even though they guess correctly, the laws of physics are still not in their favor. Hard data indicates that goalies stop only 18 percent of penalty kicks.

The goalkeeper guesses right on this penalty kick attempt in a Series A match between AC Milan and AS Rome.

The best goalies/keepers are those who can read where they think the penalty kick might be going. They learn the stance of the player. Maybe the player puts a slight weight emphasis on his right versus left leg, and that gives the goalie a clue about where the ball might go. The most talented soccer players can already anticipate their opponent's actions up to eighty milliseconds before the opponent moves. This is partially a learned response (it is true that practice makes perfect), but is also a testament to how quickly the brain reacts. Many goalies don't even know they're doing it, but their brains are registering slight clues in the way the kicker is positioned, and those clues help the goalie guess where they'll likely kick the ball. The Brunel researchers found that the goalies were registering slight motion changes in the kicker's legs moments before his foot came in contact with the ball. Goalies were also registering slight changes in the faces of the penalty kickers—changes that gave them clues about where the ball might be kicked. This is a similar concept to football, where the quarterback's eyes are a dead giveaway regarding where he will throw the ball. It's no different in soccer.

The researchers at Brunel concluded that elite soccer athletes have finely tuned visual systems that pick up information from the kicker's body movements. Goalies that practice the most do the best.

In reality, the goalie always has to make a decision before the ball is kicked regarding where he or she will provide coverage, and no matter how quick the goalie is, this situation gives the opponent the distinct advantage. When it comes to the odds, the kicker has an exceedingly high advantage.

Kickers are also good at psyching out the goalie. Kickers know that the goalie will move before the kick, so the kicker will run up and try to entice the keeper to move a particular way, then the kicker will shoot the other way. Psych!

Researchers have actually done studies to measure the optimum place for a goalie to stand, and guess what they found? Goalies who stand right in the middle of the net have a better chance of stopping goals. Why is that? A research team in Israel measured the distribution of about 300 penalty kicks and looked at instances of where the goalie moved in each of those instances. The research team found that the best probability, or statistically the best chance, of stopping a goal happened when the goalie stayed in the center of the goal.

If you've ever watched soccer matches, you'll realize that goalies don't stand in the middle. Why not? Sports are half physical and half mental—you've probably heard the saying. Behavioral **psychologists** say that goalies feel like they need

On penalty kicks, standing in the center of the goal gives goalkeepers the best chance of stopping the ball.

to do something and not just stand there; it is a reaction that psychologists call action bias. Goalies fear standing still and looking stupid—most of us can relate to that feeling. The same Israeli team of researchers polled more than thirty goalies and asked them what they would do in the 300 penalty kick situations. Most goalies said they would dive. Interestingly, if a goalie is going to dive to stop the ball, diving from the center is the best option.

 FIFA Goes Green

Goalies who were lucky enough to play in the 2018 FIFA World Cup got the chance to play in state-of-the-art "green" stadiums in Russia: Kazan Arena, Saint Petersburg Stadium, Fisht Stadium, and Spartak Stadium. FIFA mandated that the stadiums be constructed or remodeled according to "green" environmental standards to minimize the impact of construction and maintenance of the stadiums on the surrounding area. Engineers worked to worldwide green standards like BREEAM, the UK Building Research Establishment Global, and the US-developed LEED construction standard. FIFA focused on technology to improve energy consumption, proper waste management, and emissions during transport of fans to and from the matches.

However, goalies also use mind games to exert influence on penalty takers. In short, they try to psych out the kicker. When a goalie comes forward away from the net, he is reducing the thirty-six-foot distance to the net, and that psyches out the kicker. In a study published in Psychological Science, researchers studied footage of goalies. In the overwhelming majority of cases (96 percent), goalkeepers stood very slightly off center. Why do they do this, especially when we've already established that a central position is optimum? It's all about mind games. By being slightly off center, the goalies created about a ten-centimeter (4 inch) difference between their body position and each end of the goal. Interestingly, when the goalies were polled, they thought they were in the center. In other words, they were unaware that they were standing off center and were surprised to watch their own footage proving it.

Goalkeepers will sometimes leave more space on one side or the other to entice the penalty kick taker.

Interestingly, kickers were also unaware that they were choosing the side with more space, but in 103 out of 174 goal attempts, the kickers kicked to the side where there was more space. So the psych-out worked! Just because the goalie stood off center didn't mean that they would not dive to the opposite side to stop the ball. The position and stance of the goalkeeper definitely influenced the kicker's choice of where to kick. It's simple math—they kicked to the side that had more space. The team did some computer simulations and definitively found that people do in fact notice these slight movements from off center. They may not be conscious of it, but the human eye and brain do register the goalie as slightly off center. Then the brain calculates the odds, and the kicker kicks to the side with more space in the majority of cases.

Much of the mental game can be chalked up to a concept called game theory, which suggests that opponents follow predictable patterns to try to outfox each other. World-class players like Lionel Messi and Cristiano Ronaldo are not only superb athletes, they're also very skilled at decision-making. Soccer players have to make multiple decisions at the same time. Goalies know that kickers are better kicking to one side or the other, but kickers

World-class players like Messi are not only superb athletes, they're also very skilled at decision-making.

know that the goalies know, so kickers don't always favor their stronger side. Aaagh! It can be mind-numbing, but soccer is as much a mental game as it is a physical one.

If the kicker always kicked to their stronger side, the goalie would always jump to cover that side. It is the same as bluffing at poker. The kicker sometimes picks the other side to keep the goalie uncertain. Researchers call this the equilibrium strategy—kickers choose their weaker side just often enough to psych out the goalie. Goalies do the same when blocking shots. They keep each other on their toes.

Text-Dependent Questions:

1. Why is the goalie at a disadvantage defending the soccer net?

2. What is game theory?

3. What factors affect reaction time?

Research Project:

Put game theory to the test. Get two friends to go with you to the soccer field. One of you will play goalie, and one will play kicker. The third person will record data in a notebook. The two players should use game theory strategy to try to psych each other out. How many times did the goalie guess correctly regarding where the ball would be kicked? How many times was it missed? Even better would be to record your session to review later. As a group, go over your observations. How did game theory factor in?

CHAPTER 4

THE STATS

Wow! Who knew there was so much math involved in watching a soccer match? These days, pretty much every possible part of a soccer match can be measured. There are **statistics** on each player, each team, and each league. Fans can even compare stats between teams. Here are some of the categories of statistics that are measured.

Count Statistics

The simplest statistics measured are simple counts, such as number of games played by a team or a single player, number of games started by a player, or number of goals or game-winning goals scored by a team or player. Statisticians even measure things like the number of assists, meaning the passes that led to a goal, and how many shots at the goal were attempted. When a player gets three goals in a single game, it is referred to as a "hat trick," and these are counted as well.

Players who score three goals in a match are credited with what is called a "hat trick".

Time Statistics

Soccer has many statistics that measure time, such as minutes played by a particular player. Time of possession per team and overtime minutes (meaning the number of minutes played in the extra period) are among the time stats that are tracked.

Fantasy Futbol

Fantasy football and basketball exist, but did you know that fantasy MLS soccer also exists? Fans use the previously mentioned statistics and **analytics** to look at each player to create a dream team of MLS defenders, forwards, midfielders, and keepers. It can be really fun to gather a group of friends together to analyze all the player data and pick your own dream team. After each person picks his or her team, your fantasy teams compete against each other. You use stats from each player on your dream team to see who has the best record at the end of the season. Bet you never knew how much math goes into fantasy soccer!

Ratio Statistics

After individual counts and times are measured, it is possible to combine these measurements into **ratio** measurements. For example, shooting percentage is measured in soccer, meaning the ratio of goals scored to shots taken. Save ratio is also measured, indicating the goalie's number of saves to goals. These measurements are often indicated in straight ratios or in percentages.

Averages

Measurements of averages can show consistency of a team's or player's performance over the whole season. For example, GAA, or goals against average, can be measured to track the number of goals allowed per game on average. The formula is (GA*90)/minutes, or the goals per game multiplied by 90 minutes and then divided by the number of minutes the team had possession of the ball. The same formula is used to calculate the number of saves per game.

Goals against average and time of possession are just a couple of the statistics that are tracked in soccer.

Cautions

You might have heard of the terms "yellow card" or "red card" in a soccer game, but do you know what they mean? Sometimes the referee holds up either a yellow or a red card after a play. Yellow cards are caution cards, meaning the referee is cautioning the player regarding their actions on the field. After a player receives two yellow cards, they automatically earn a red card. A red card is an ejection card, meaning the player is ejected from the game for not properly following the rules. The team is then short one player for the remainder of the game. Additionally, the team gets a direct or indirect kick every time the referee shows a yellow or red card.

How Statistics Apply to Soccer

When a player commits a foul, the referee determines if it is serious enough to warrant being cautioned (yellow card) or ejected (red card) from the match.

 Text Dependent Questions:

1. Can you give five examples of soccer statistics that are based on counts?

2. How does a yellow card differ from a red card?

3. What is a hat trick?

 Research Project:

Choose your favorite MLS soccer team or international team. Locate websites that report statistics, and record them for two weeks in each of the following categories: time, ratios, averages, penalties, counts. How did the team compare from week to week? Did it improve, stay the same, or get worse?

WORDS TO UNDERSTAND

agility: the ability to move quickly in a coordinated fashion

parry: to knock away

plyometrics: repeated rapid stretching exercises, like jumping and rebounding, used to contract muscles to increase muscle power

CHAPTER 5

TRAINING AND FITNESS

Many soccer coaches take soccer training back to the basics to develop their players' **agility** and speed. Like any sport, soccer takes consistency, hard work, repetition, and a drive to improve your skills. Here are some of the equipment and drills that the pros use.

Agility and Flexibility

Agility exercises are designed as short-duration, high-intensity activities. An extensive body of research shows that these types of drills increase strength, power, balance, and coordination. They are also great fat-burning exercises as well because of the high intensity.

But how do these exercises work to transform your body? Agility training works by improving your rate of muscle contraction. It also improves your stationary balance, dynamic balance (meaning your balance while you are in motion), and overall coordination. Improvements in these movements enhance your natural reflexes, which in turn improves your reaction time.

For example, agility ladder exercises strengthen the tendons, ligaments, and joints, and provide a great workout for your

Agility ladder drills improve speed, quickness and cardiovascular function along with agility.

heart, too. Pretty soon, you'll have improved cardio function, but you'll notice that your knees lift higher and your foot strikes in and out of the ladder rungs are faster. That's agility training, and it works! A study published in the *Journal of Strength and Conditioning Research* even found that agility training helps improve cognitive performance and memory because it forces you to focus and learn various movement patterns. Your coaches want you to do these drills without looking down at the ladder, so your muscles and your brain are learning something new. Be sure to switch up your routine to work out different muscles.

Soccer cones can be set out on the field for various footwork drills and agility workouts. For example, agility cones are about a foot high and are used in warm-ups, and speed and agility drills. Coaches often use speed ladders—several sets of them, in fact—during practice to lay out on the field for use in drills to increase your speed. Every coach will have a stopwatch out on the field to get accurate times to measure your speed improvement. Coaches can also use agility poles; these are simple straight poles that stick into the ground. The coach will ask you to weave around them in various drill and running patterns to increase your agility and speed during workouts.

Work It Like Beckham

What does David Beckham's workout look like? He certainly gets a lot of exercise running around on the soccer field, but he also puts in a lot of time in the gym. Beckham does both indoor and outdoor workouts. He does less weightlifting to avoid building bulk and more cardio workouts that are high intensity to increase heart rate. He also uses sixty-yard turnarounds—run sixty yards at full sprint, turn around, run back at full sprint, rest for one minute, and repeat. He also uses **plyometrics** to increase agility, core abdominal strength, quickness, and speed. He said he did eight to ten reps of this exercise daily, which is why he never appeared out of breath during a match. He also credits good nutrition like chicken and vegetables with keeping his lean physique.

Soccer players need to develop and maintain strength and flexibility, so resistance bands (long rubber bands) are a must-have piece of equipment. These bands come in different colors representing different amounts of tension and are used for different types of workouts. The bands actually serve to lengthen individual muscle fibers so that the player develops more flexibility over time.

A good pair of soccer cleats is essential to maintain good footing out on the field.

Every player needs a good pair of soccer cleats and a good pair of running shoes. Soccer players also need great balance, so coaches use a stability disc, which is a rubber disk that you stand on to help your balance. Trainers often use these in rehabilitation after an injury.

Check out these amazing soccer-training drills at the Hoffenheim training facility in Germany.

Soccer coaches and trainers also use those famously heavy medicine balls for soccer strength and conditioning drills, as well as rehabilitation. A five- or ten-pound ball will do. Exercise balls are also used in soccer. These are large inflated balls that are used to strengthen core abdominal muscles.

You can use some really cool equipment to help build your kicking skills. For example, a portable player wall can be set up on any blank gym or outdoor wall. The portable wall simulates a free kick game situation and is used to practice those kicks.

Improving Reaction Time

If you're a goalie, you probably already have pretty good reflexes and reaction times. On average, a typical reaction time is around 0.2 to 0.3 second. The best goalies have a reaction time under 0.2 second. What's yours? And how do you get better?

Although reaction time is largely dependent on genetics, it is possible to train and improve it by as much as 20 percent. Better reaction times help with all types of reaction saves, including dives, punches, and tips over the bar. Coaches want the goalie to get to the point where they can make reaction saves really without even thinking, and lots of dynamic drills are available that can help.

Dynamic drills help to improve the reaction time of goalkeepers.

It is not always best, or possible, for goalies to catch the ball, so they include drills to parry, or punch, the ball in their training.

One is tossing the soccer ball over your head to a partner. It sounds simple, but it really works. Another drill involves rolling the ball around your feet in a figure-eight pattern.

Lots of soccer players use a technique called overspeed training. By reacting to something faster than a soccer ball, you are tuning your reaction time. For example, soccer players might use a pitching machine that throws a baseball at 130 to 150 miles per hour. Your brain adapts to catching the fast-moving baseball, so when you return to the soccer field, the soccer ball is now slower by comparison, and you have faster reflexes.

Most soccer teams do simulation exercises where a kicker calls the shot as left, right, or center, and the goalie quickly reacts to stop the shot. Some coaches insist on over-the-rope training. They hold a rope at knee height and extend it out from the goal in a straight line with the netting on the side. The goalie will jump over the rope, shoulder-roll on the ground, stand up, and stop the shot just after the feet are planted.

Many goalies also work on reaction time by doing hand and foot drills. A kicker stands about five yards out, and the goalie quickly stops the balls as they are kicked in quick succession. Goalies can better learn to **parry** when soccer balls are sent in rapid-fire succession, one right after the other. Use tennis balls for this drill—if you can stop the smaller ball, you will definitely be able to stop a soccer ball!

Text Dependent Questions:

1. Name two ways to improve agility.

2. How does agility differ from flexibility?

3. Is reaction time completely dependent on genetics, or can the body be trained to react faster?

Research Project:

Do your own reaction-time measurements. You'll need a ruler, paper, and pencil. Have a person stand next to you and drop the ruler between a count of one to five. Catch the ruler as quickly as you can by pinching it between your fingers. In general, 100 milliseconds translates into about two inches or five centimeters, so you can measure your reaction time. Add distractions like loud noises, or create a visual disturbance by turning a flashlight on and off. Do these distractions make a difference?

An alternative to using the ruler is to use an online reaction test like this one: https://www.humanbenchmark.com/tests/reactiontime

On average, reaction times are about 150 to 300 milliseconds. It's amazing to think of all the calculations and data processing the brain is making during that time. The eyes see the ruler falling, and then the eyes send that information from sensory cells called neurons to the brain's visual cortex, which translates what you are seeing. Then, the brain has to send a signal to your hand to catch the ruler. There's a lot happening in under a half second.

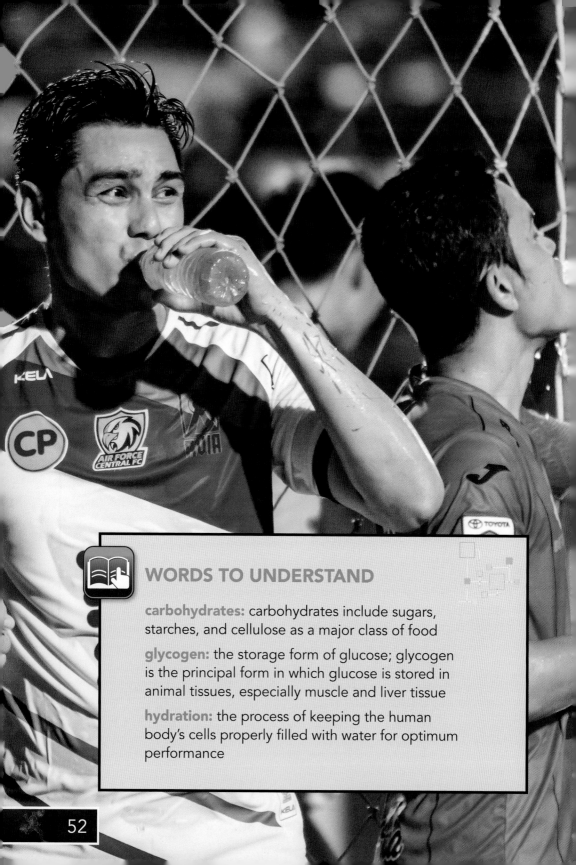

WORDS TO UNDERSTAND

carbohydrates: carbohydrates include sugars, starches, and cellulose as a major class of food

glycogen: the storage form of glucose; glycogen is the principal form in which glucose is stored in animal tissues, especially muscle and liver tissue

hydration: the process of keeping the human body's cells properly filled with water for optimum performance

CHAPTER 6

NUTRITION

Good nutrition is important for every person but particularly so for athletes because it is so closely linked to performance. Most athletes need to eat significantly more calories than the average person, but they must be the right calories to provide fuel for the muscles. In general, athletes need 2,000 to 5,000 calories per day; the amount varies by body size and gender. An athlete without good nutrition will definitely see a negative impact on his or her health and athletic performance.

Energy

The right balance of proteins, healthy fats, and **carbohydrates** provides the fuel bodies need to maintain energy during a workout or soccer match. For example, carbohydrates, protein, and healthy fats provide the fuel needed to maintain energy. Carbohydrates regulate both blood sugar and **glycogen** levels in the muscles, so you have to have enough carbs to prevent muscle fatigue. Contrary to popular belief, athletes do need fats for energy. Severe restrictions like a very low-fat diet are the worst thing you can do. Fats break down into fatty acids, which your body needs as an energy source for long workouts and matches. Glucose and carbs burn first, but after that, fatty

High-protein foods like meat, eggs, and nuts help build muscle, and are also good energy sources.

acids provide up to 75 percent of the energy that athletes need for longer-duration performances. In short, fats provide endurance. Proteins contain building blocks called amino acids, which are essential to help your body build new muscle tissue. Proteins are also a great energy source.

 Food Library

Did you know that the US government's Department of Agriculture has a National Agricultural Library? It is located in Beltsville, Maryland, near Washington, DC. It has many online resources specific for athlete nutrition, including proper nutrition during exercise, healthy weight control methods for teen athletes, a guide to eating for sports, and much more. Visit the library at https://www.nal.usda.gov/fnic/nutrition-athletes.

Weight Control

Athletes definitely need to maintain a healthy weight, and good nutrition will help you reach that goal. Don't restrict calories or proteins or fats if you need to lose weight. These restrictions will negatively impact your performance and are also dangerous. If you're trying to lose weight, get full on healthy foods like fruits and high-fiber vegetables that fill you up in a nutritious way to ensure you get all the essential nutrients your body needs while losing weight. Be sure to eat lean meats and other proteins and lower-fat dairy products. Look to authorities like The American College of Sports Medicine for expert advice and guidance, or see a registered dietician who will design an eating plan for your needs.

Soccer players must maintain an optimal level of hydration to perform at their best.

Hydration

Athletes know that a vital element of training is maintaining good **hydration**. The human body is largely composed of water, so an inability to maintain a proper fluid balance will adversely affect your performance and create a risk for dehydration. Did you know that water makes up more than 60 percent of the human body? A fluid loss of just 1 percent of your body weight can have negative effects on your endurance and your cardiovascular function. Unfortunately, your body doesn't usually perceive a problem until 2 or 3 percent of your body water is lost. You will get thirsty at that point, but by

Soccer players should ideally drink about three liters of water each day.

then, both your physical performance and cognitive function are likely to be impaired.

What's more, researchers from the University of Utah found that a similar level of dehydration (2–3 percent) could depress metabolic rate. In one study, participants were given four, eight, or twelve 8-ounce glasses of water a day. On the fifth day, the researchers found that the folks drinking only four glasses of water per day were modestly dehydrated and their metabolic rates had decreased significantly. The participants who drank eight or twelve glasses of water were adequately hydrated, had more energy, were able to concentrate better, and burned calories at an accelerated rate (compared to the folks who drank four glasses per day).

Not only that, water intake may have a direct positive impact on your fat-loss efforts by something that researchers refer to as "preloading," which simply refers to drinking water before meals.

Certainly as an athlete, you need plenty of water when you're training or playing outdoors in hot and humid conditions, but it is important to remember that dehydration can occur in any environment. Plain water is the best choice

The Renegade Pharmacist shows you exactly what diet soda does to your body!

Just because a sweet-tasting drink is sugar free does not make it better for you. Artificial sweeteners found in diet drinks are even worse than sugar.

for staying hydrated, but if you are intensely sweating, consider water with electrolytes or a sports drink to replace lost electrolytes. Just remember that some so-called healthy sports drinks have as much sugar as a soda, so read labels and choose a drink with a lower sugar content.

For most teenagers, soda is a big dietary culprit. In fact, soda is the single biggest calorie source for Americans. On average, most Americans drink two cans every day. That's a lot of sugar! It goes without saying—don't use soda to rehydrate. Sodas greatly affect your performance on the field. The high sugar content makes your body work even harder and zaps your energy. Complex sugars like high fructose corn syrup change the way your brain recognizes how much sugar you are actually eating or drinking. These complex sugars make your brain become leptin-resistant. Leptin is the protein that regulates how much energy you take in and expend. When you drink a sugary soda, you don't feel full, even though you've just ingested high amounts of sugar. This throws your leptin regulation off balance in a big way and over time can lead to you adding fat onto your body.

Now, you might be thinking, "Well, I drink diet soda, so that's better for me because it has no sugar and no calories." There are many kids who think just like you do; kids are now consuming diet soda twice as much as they did ten years ago.

Think again. Diet soda has its own set of problems that impact not only your sports performance but also your health. Here are just a few of the health issues that come with popping the top on a diet soda can:

◇ Kidney Problems: Diet soda is really bad for your kidneys. Studies have shown that when people drink more than two diet sodas per day, their kidney function begins declining.

◇ Metabolism Mix-up: Diet soda really messes with your metabolism. Even one can a day can lead to a much higher incidence of metabolic syndrome, a condition of increased cholesterol and added belly fat.

◇ Obesity: Diet soda does not help you lose weight. The more diet soda you drink, the more you risk becoming overweight. The artificial sweeteners in diet soda disrupt the body's ability to regulate sweetness, so people tend to overeat.

◇ Cell Damage: Diet sodas contain preservatives like sodium and potassium benzoates that can cause DNA damage, asthma, hives, and other allergies.

◇ Tooth Damage: With a pH of 3.2, diet soda is very acidic. By comparison, water has a pH of 7, but soda is closer to battery acid with a pH of 1. Yikes! Over time, the acid will dissolve your tooth enamel. Dentists say that soda drinkers by far have much more tooth decay and other issues.

Most teens do not stay sufficiently hydrated in general, and if you're an athlete, it is even easier to become dehydrated. After all, hydration helps your body successfully perform and your muscles to recover from workouts. At school, keep a water bottle with you throughout the day to help stay hydrated. If you're thirsty, that is a sign that you are already becoming dehydrated. The rule of thumb is to drink three liters of no- or low-calorie drinks per day, ideally water, and avoid artificial sweeteners.

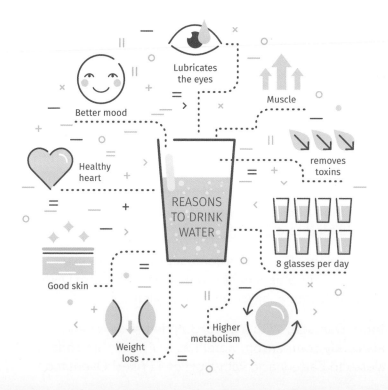

Top Nutritional Advice from the Experts

Have you ever wondered what elite athletes do in terms of nutrition? Many teams offer their players nutritional education so they can learn for themselves what true, proper nutrition is—and what it isn't. You might be thinking that you can't possibly learn the same things they know. After all, they have trainers, dieticians, and other experts on the team to help and teach them.

Certainly, nutritional science is complex, but there are some easy-to-follow guidelines for healthy eating that are good for anyone to use, whether or not you're an athlete.

There are three top nutrition rules that all athletes follow. Rule 1 is called the 80/20 rule, meaning that 80 percent of the time, they choose the foods that are best for their bodies. Each meal and snack is properly chosen to provide the best in nutrition and fuel. The other 20 percent of the time, athletes cheat a little bit. They eat their favorites, like a big greasy hamburger or a big bowl of macaroni and cheese. These foods may not be the best choice nutritionally, but they are the athlete's favorite food. The theory is that eating what you like for 20 percent of the time helps you stay on track the other 80 percent of the time.

Rule 2 is that athletes get enough sleep. Most aim for eight hours, but if that isn't possible, get as much as you can—at least six or seven hours—and don't be afraid to sneak in short power naps when you can. While we are asleep, the body recovers and repairs itself, even if you doze off for fifteen minutes. Your metabolism won't properly function

The phrase "eat a rainbow" means that a healthy diet should contain plenty of fruits and vegetables, many of which are brightly colored.

without proper sleep. Two hormones called ghrelin and leptin are involved. If you sleep only five hours instead of eight hours each night, your body will produce more ghrelin, the "go" hormone that your body produces when you're awake. Ghrelin tells your body to eat. Leptin, on the other hand, is the hormone that tells you to stop eating, so if you sleep less, you have less leptin. If you're sleepy during the day, you're also much more likely to make poor food choices, like eating sugary foods to get an energy spike or consuming caffeine to stay awake. Then you get worse sleep, and you produce more ghrelin. It is a vicious cycle, so be sure to catch some zzzzzs.

Rule 3 is to "eat a rainbow." No, we don't mean literally. Instead, the phrase "eat a rainbow" means to eat fruits and vegetables at every meal and at snack time too. The rainbow refers to eating a wide variety of colors—blueberries and strawberries at breakfast, red or green apples for a snack, cucumbers and carrots for lunch, and lots of leafy greens and other vegetables for dinner.

All athletes should also remember the following important nutritional rules:

◇ Don't eat processed foods. Choose items with the least amount of processing, like fruits, vegetables, and whole grains.

◇ Choose lean proteins for each meal.

◇ Every diet needs healthy fats like nuts, avocados, fish, seeds, olive oil, and natural nut butters like peanut or cashew butter.

◇ Always, always, always eat breakfast, and be sure to eat something within thirty minutes of waking up. You'll definitely give a good start to your metabolism, and you'll have more energy as the day goes on.

◇ Rather than eating three big meals every day, break your meals into smaller portions and eat more often. Spread four to six meals over the entire day. Ideally, you should be eating every three hours for optimal athlete fuel.

◇ After a workout, you should always have a small meal or shake that is a combination of carbs and protein. Many athletes refer to not eating after a workout as "wasting a workout." Why? Because exercise actually does deplete your muscles of fuel as well as causing some minor damage, so your muscle needs repair. These small changes in the muscle are actually beneficial because as the muscles repair after each workout, they get better after the exercise

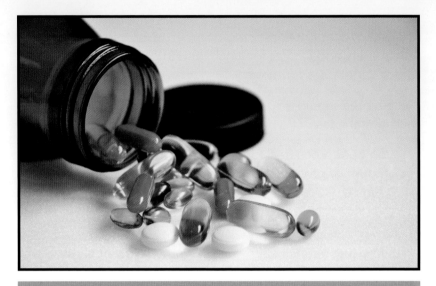

Athletes should not use vitamin supplements as a substitute for good nutrition.

demands are placed on them. Muscle becomes depleted for only a short time. Then it builds a stronger and more aerobic capability. Basically, your body is tearing down weaker muscle fibers and building stronger ones. But you've got to give those rebuilding muscles good nutrition.

◇ Don't use vitamins as a substitute for poor nutrition. Get what you need through your food, adding multivitamins as a supplement. Check with a doctor or dietician regarding what supplements are right for you.

◇ Nutrition is just as much a concern after the game as it is before the game, so make it a priority. Hydration is definitely a big part of this. The majority of athletes don't get enough fluid or fuel for energy during soccer matches, so restoring these depleted nutrients after the game is very beneficial and essential. Since you've lost electrolytes during the match, eat high-sodium foods like cheese and soups. Ideally, you should eat a small meal of carbs, fat, and protein thirty minutes after the game. Of course, sometimes this is not possible, so pack a snack of bananas (to replenish potassium), apples, and whole-grain bagels or breads.

Text-Dependent Questions:

1. Describe what the phrase "eat a rainbow" means to you.
2. Name the top three nutrition rules that athletes follow.
3. What is the first sign that you might be dehydrated?

Research Project:

Track your meals for one week, recording what you have for breakfast, lunch, dinner, and snacks. Are you following the 80/20 rule, or were you more like 70/30? Is there a pattern for when you ate the 20 percent of "cheat" foods? Was it on the weekend or during the week when you were tired after soccer practice? Dieticians will tell you that when you have a written record of what you eat, you definitely are better able to stick to the eating plan. If you cook, or your parents cook dinner, take the regular recipe and see if you can substitute healthier ingredients, such as low-fat milk instead of regular milk, lean meats like chicken instead of fatty meats, and other substitutions. Was the recipe just as good with the substitutions? Compare notes with friends or team members. Can you borrow from each other's healthy habits?

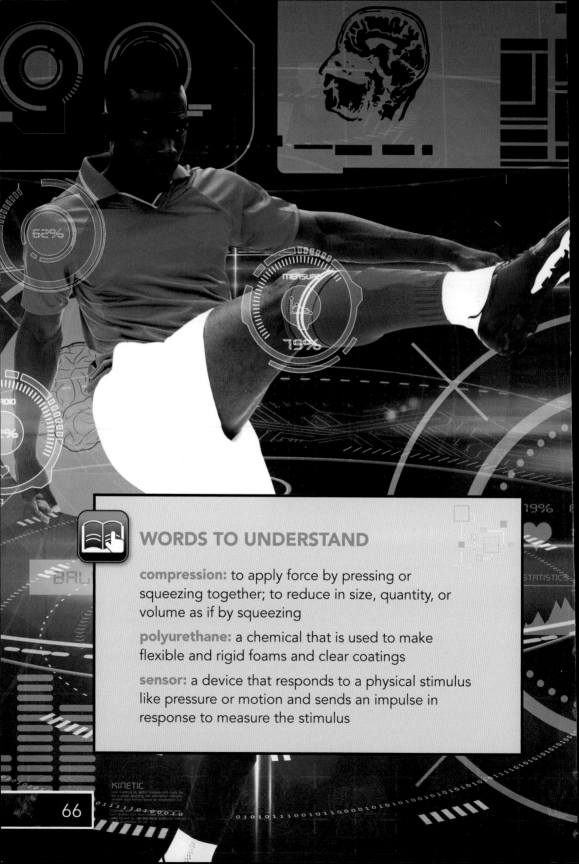

WORDS TO UNDERSTAND

compression: to apply force by pressing or squeezing together; to reduce in size, quantity, or volume as if by squeezing

polyurethane: a chemical that is used to make flexible and rigid foams and clear coatings

sensor: a device that responds to a physical stimulus like pressure or motion and sends an impulse in response to measure the stimulus

CHAPTER 7

HIGH-TECH SOCCER

The wonderful world of sports definitely has some of the coolest high-tech gear. Here are some of the latest gadgets and gizmos that soccer athletes, coaches, and trainers are using to gather and analyze data for better coaching and better athlete preparation on and off the soccer field.

Apparel

Gloves

A soccer ball can fly toward the net (and the goalie) at ninety miles per hour. That's fast! As you can imagine, your hands would really hurt if you tried to catch that ball without wearing gloves. Goalies today not only wear gloves, they wear really cool high-tech gloves. For one thing, these gloves have plastic spines inserted in them to add structural support. The spines fit behind each finger and the thumb to keep fingers from bending backward when the goalie makes those amazing catches. The spines also help put the hand in the proper ergonomic position, with fingers already splayed out. The engineers have analyzed data on hand breaks in soccer athletes and have provided extra protection on those areas of the glove. For example, the gloves add extra protection to the wrist bone. The palm of the gloves contains foam like memory foam that goes into **compression** on impact to absorb energy. The material of the glove helps the player regardless of whether they're playing in wet or dry conditions or on hard ground or soft grass. The inside of the glove is covered in a latex material that helps the keeper better grasp and hold onto the ball, and the gloves are meshed for venting and air flow for better comfort.

Soccer goalie gloves are reinforced to protect the goalkeeper's fingers from bending too far.

Jerseys

You've heard of smartphones, but did you know that soccer now has smart jerseys? The jersey is made to be very tight fitting to build compression right in. Elastic bands around the ribcage and shoulders add extra support.

Shin guards

If you've been kicked in the shin, you know how much that hurts. Today's shin guards provide amazing protection and are very lightweight—all at the same time. How do they do it? A thick layer of foam molds to the shin and leg, whereas a **polyurethane** cover adds triple protection. Old shin guards were bulky, but newer models are form-fitted to the curve of the leg.

Cleats

Companies like Adidas and others make a "smart cleat" that contains a tracking device to measure just about everything—speed, distance, number of steps, stride rates, and sprint times. The embedded chip can store that data for seven hours, and you can download it over Wi-Fi or on a USB device. Wow! You can download the data into an app

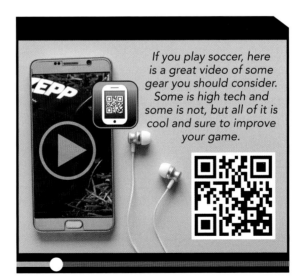

If you play soccer, here is a great video of some gear you should consider. Some is high tech and some is not, but all of it is cool and sure to improve your game.

and even share your data on Facebook. Coaches can upload the data into a personalized training plan for each player. A cavity in the outer sole houses the tiny chip. Data is recorded every second.

VAR

VAR, or Video Assistant Referee, is an official that assists the on-field crew at professional matches with decisions on goals, penalties or red cards. The on-field crew must request this assistance. When called upon, the VAR has access to several video replays from multiple angles provided by cameras located all around the field, including in the goalposts. If the VAR locates a clear error, the on-field referee is notified and then he or she reviews the play at a sideline monitor station, and the referee then decides on the call.

Equipment

Ah, the elusive design of the perfect soccer ball. How does a designer create that perfect surface? Many have tried. Some soccer balls are now heat-bonded rather than stitched together to create better airflow around the ball. Ball manufacturers have been experimenting with the number of hexagons. Rather than the traditional thirty-two hexagonal panels, balls can be made of eight, fourteen, or sixteen panels. In the 2010 World Cup, the Jabulani ball design was used; it had just eight panels, all spherically molded and thermally bonded. The Jabulani ball wasn't perfectly smooth, but it certainly didn't have the typical rough surface of a standard thirty-two-panel design either. Players found the ball frustrating to play with—it had an unpredictable and erratic flight path that varied depending on the speed at which it was kicked.

The on-field referee at a 2018 match in Lubin, Poland, makes use of the replay system after calling for help from the VAR.

After the tournament, NASA researchers actually studied the Jabulani's aerodynamics. The NASA engineers saw the same thing the players experienced—an erratic and asymmetrical flight path. NASA's official ruling was that the ball was unpredictable.

Companies are trying to produce the most perfectly round ball and the most aerodynamic one. Many soccer balls now come texturized for better grip.

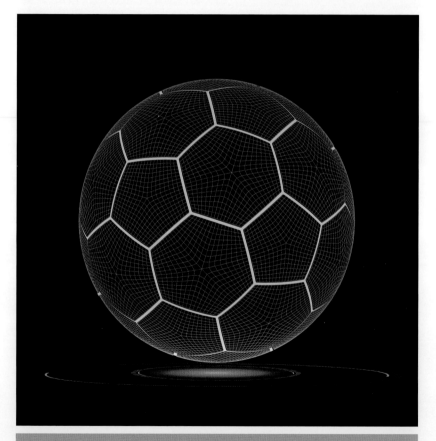

Engineers are constantly tinkering with the design of the soccer ball to come up with the best version.

High-Tech Stadiums:

Tech geeks, rejoice! Soccer stadiums are becoming very high-tech. The home stadium of the MLS San Jose Earthquakes is Avaya Stadium in California. The high-speed Wi-Fi–enabled stadium comes complete with cloud technology and its own mobile app that fans can use to do everything—buy food, park, pay for tickets, tweet, and get player stats. LED video screens are located throughout the stadium and show athlete videos, player statistics, and live fan tweets. As in California, MLS fans in Kansas can also go high-tech. Sporting Park in Kansas City has an app where fans can live-stream the game from seven different camera angles. Now, that's cool. Wembley Stadium in England is a famous soccer stadium, and it has also gone high-tech. An app provides fans with news feeds, video and audio of the match, pictures, and even an interactive stadium map for fans to find their seats. The app even has a travel planner to help fans get to and from various parts of the UK to Wembley Stadium.

Perhaps the coolest ball of all is the smart ball. Yes, that's right--now soccer balls come embedded with a **sensor** that measures data like speed, flight path, and spin. It's amazing. Big companies like Wilson and Adidas are making soccer balls with these sensors, but so are small start-up companies, too. The data is sent real-time to a smartphone or tablet app for instant feedback. The ball is easy to recharge, and the charge can usually last for a whole week of practice. The smart chip tracks all kinds of performance data, like ball trajectory and shot accuracy. Some of the apps are so sophisticated they use real-time ball tracking to give you a grade on how well you did on your footwork. You can even practice skills in front of a screen; it's like a virtual personalized trainer. Some

German sporting goods giant Adidas has developed a smart ball containing an integrated sensor system.

have hundreds of soccer drills you can choose based on your skill level, and you get a grade at the end of each workout drill. The app is designed for casual players all the way up to professionals.

It took Adidas engineers more than four years to research all the science that went into their smart soccer ball. It looks exactly like a regular FIFA soccer ball on the outside, but it has an integrated sensor system inside that measures all the data. The ball is super durable. Adidas says it can survive 7,000 sixty-mile-per-hour kicks. Now, that's durable.

 Text-Dependent Questions:

1. What is the purpose of the embedded plastic spines in gloves?

2. How many hexagonal panels did the Jabulani ball design have?

3. Why are soccer ball manufacturers experimenting with designs that have different numbers of hexagonal panels?

 Research Project:

Choose a piece of soccer equipment—cleats, ball, gloves—whatever your favorite is. Design it to be as high-tech as possible. Make a list of features you're creating and the purpose behind each feature. Make a list of materials you would use to create the design.

SERIES GLOSSARY OF KEY TERMS

Acceleration - the rate of change of velocity with respect to time.

Aerodynamics - the branch of mechanics that deals with the motion of air and other gases and with the effects of such motion on bodies in the medium.

Algorithm - a set of rules for solving a problem in a finite number of steps.

Amplitude - the absolute value of the maximum displacement from a zero value during one period of an oscillation.

Analytics - the analysis of data, typically large sets of business data, by the use of mathematics, statistics, and computer software.

Biometrics - Methods for differentiating humans based upon one or more intrinsic physical or behavioral traits such as fingerprints or facial geometry.

Center of Gravity - the point at which the entire weight of a body may be considered as concentrated so that if supported at this point the body would remain in equilibrium in any position.

Force - strength or energy exerted or brought to bear.

Geometry - the part of mathematics concerned with the size, shape, and relative position of figures, or the study of lines, angles, shapes, and their properties.

Inertia - the property of matter by which it retains its state of rest or its velocity along a straight line so long as it is not acted upon by an external force.

Kinetic energy - energy associated with motion.

Mass - the quantity of matter as determined from its weight.

Parabola - a type of conic section curve, any point of which is equally distant from a fixed focus point and a fixed straight line.

Potential energy - the energy of a body or system as a result of its position in an electric, magnetic, or gravitational field.

Velocity - rapidity of motion or operation; swiftness; speed.

FURTHER READING

Critchley, Simon. *What We Think about When We Think about Soccer.* New York, Penguin Books, 2017.

Hoena, Blake. *National Geographic Kids Everything Soccer: Score Tons of Photos, Facts, and Fun.* 2014.

Irlen, Helen. *Sports Concussions and Getting Back in the Game . . . of Life: A Solution for Concussion Symptoms Including Headaches, Light Sensitivity, Poor Academic Performance, Anxiety and Others.* 2016

Minton, Roland B. *Sports Math: An Introductory Course in the Mathematics of Sports Science and Sports Analytics.* Boca Raton, FL: Chapman and Hall/CRC, 2016.

Part, Michael. *The Amazing Story of Leo Messi.* California: Sole Books, 2013.

INTERNET RESOURCES

FIFA
The website of soccer's international governing body
Website: https://www.fifa.com/faq.html

US Soccer Federation
The website of soccer's governing body in the United States
Website: https://www.ussoccer.com/

American Youth Soccer Organization
AYSO National Office
One of the sport's youth soccer organizations
Website: https://ayso.org/

United States Power Soccer Organization
Website: https://www.powersoccerusa.org/

American Soccer League
Website: http://www.aslsoccer.org/

North American Soccer League
Website: http://www.nasl.com/

INDEX

INDEX

AUTHOR BIOGRAPHY

Jacqueline Havelka is a rocket scientist turned writer. She is a biomedical engineer with a degree from Texas A&M University, and worked at Lockheed Martin as an aerospace contractor for the NASA Johnson Space Center in Houston, Texas. In her twenty-five-year career, she managed space life sciences experiments and data for the International Space Station and Space Shuttle. She began work on Shuttle mission STS-40 and worked until the last Shuttle launch of STS-135. While at NASA, she served in technical lead and management roles. She was a charter designer of the NASA Life Sciences Data Archive, a repository of NASA human, animal, and biological research from the Gemini program to present day.

In 2017, she founded her own company to provide medical and technical freelance writing to clients. She has always had the desire to start her own business, and she loves the challenge and diversity of international projects that her new business brings. She learns something new every single day, and that is a very good thing.

EDUCATIONAL VIDEO LINKS

Pg. 12: http://x-qr.net/1Efa
Pg. 20: http://x-qr.net/1GzC
Pg. 30: http://x-qr.net/1FBp
Pg. 42: http://x-qr.net/1F15

Pg. 48: http://x-qr.net/1Gyr
Pg. 57: http://x-qr.net/1FRg
Pg. 69: http://x-qr.net/1HSx

PICTURE CREDITS